Kirkcaldy

Then & Now

Carol McNeill

CW00536144

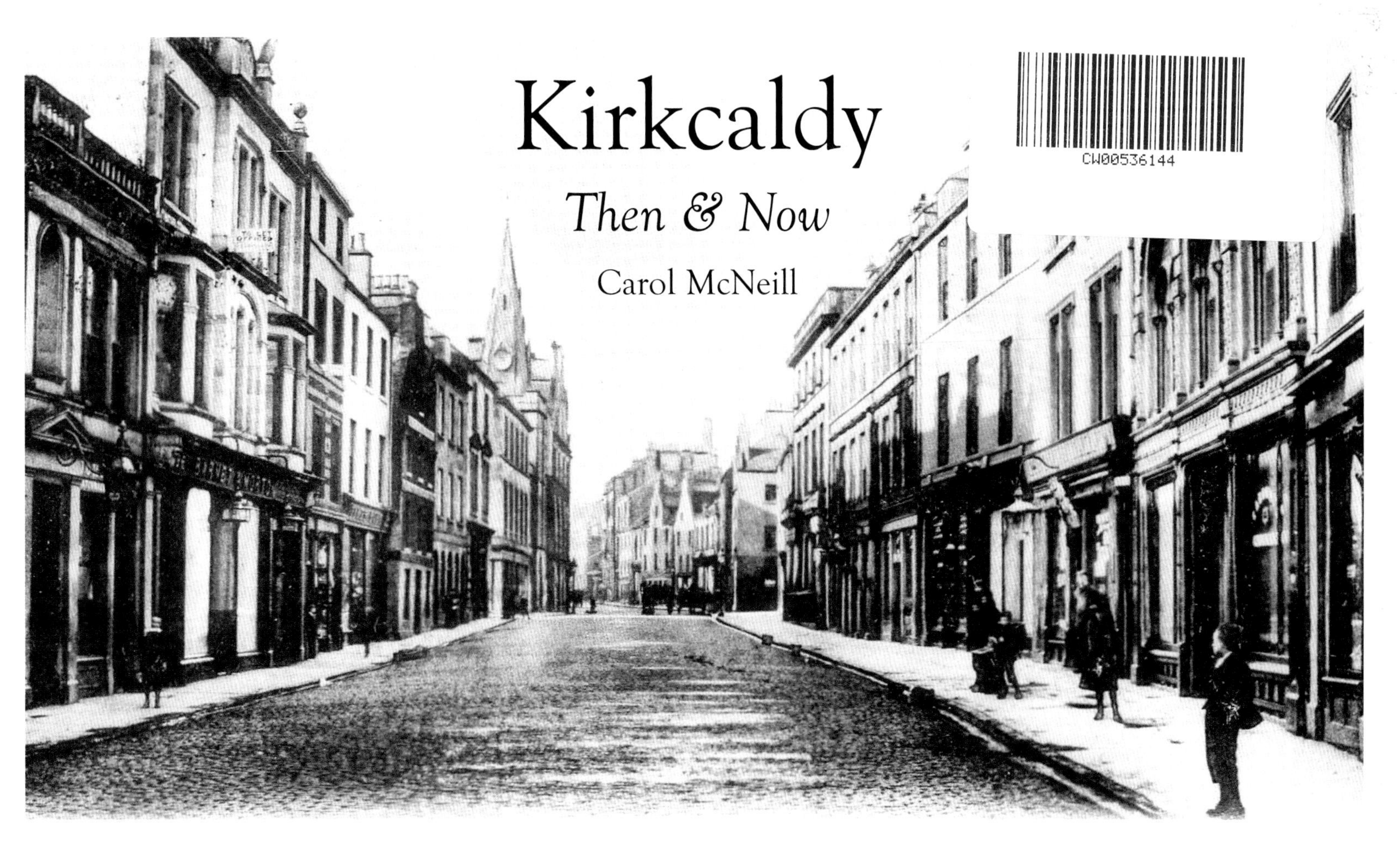

This early image of Kirkcaldy High Street in 1902 looking west shows the Town Hall which was built in 1827 with an imposing steeple, clock and bell and which replaced an even earlier building. It included the Council Chamber on the first floor which was hung with oil paintings of local provosts. Events including the proclamation of Edward VII's accession to the throne in 1901 took place outside. It was demolished in 1935 and replaced by the current building in Wemyssfield at the Town Square which was completed in 1953. Marks and Spencer's store stands on the site with a commemorative plaque erected by Kirkcaldy Civic Society. Although the High Street has altered dramatically, some architectural features including the arched first-floor windows on the right and the stone eagles just visible on the rooftop on the left still remain.

Text © Carol McNeill, 2016.
First published in the United Kingdom, 2016,
by Stenlake Publishing Ltd.
Telephone: 01290 551122
www.stenlake.co.uk

ISBN 9781840337679

The publishers regret that they cannot supply copies of any pictures featured in this book.

Acknowledgements

The author would like to thank the following for the generous loan of images and supply of information, and for their patience in answering endless queries about old Kirkcaldy: Carr's Hutchison's Mills, Fife Ports Authority, Jim Fraser, Bob Kilgour, Kirkcaldy Civic Society, Local History staff at Kirkcaldy Galleries, Pearl McLachlan, Don Swanson, and Eddie Wellcoat.

Introduction

Kirkcaldy was often known as the Lang Toun because of its long High Street which runs roughly parallel to the esplanade. Linktown in the west and Pathhead, Gallatown and Dysart further east were originally separate burghs which ran their own affairs, but which were incorporated into the burgh in 1876 and (in the case of Dysart) 1930. The built environment of the town has changed tremendously over the last hundred years or so, with housing and new infrastructure stretching further and further in most directions. The once green fields of farms such as Hayfield and Bogie Mains, and the lush estates of Raith and Dunnikier have largely given way to housing developments.

The town has long been associated with the manufacture of linoleum, one of its main industries. Indeed its distinctive odour gave rise to the famous lines from the 1913 poem, *The Boy in the Train*, by Mary Campbell Smith: 'For I ken mysel' by the queer like smell, that the next stop's Kirkcaddy!' Michael Nairn & Co. Ltd. and competitors Barry, Ostlere and Shepherd Ltd. had several manufacturing plants producing linoleum which gave employment to very large numbers of people and which was exported virtually worldwide.

There were of course other main industries – looking back now, an almost unbelievable selection – which included linen mills, flax spinning, bleaching, flour mills and maltings, potteries, ship building, engineering and coal mining, with the harbour constantly busy with a vibrant import and export trade. Kirkcaldy Harbour was one of the most important factors in bringing the town from a small coastal settlement to a thriving industrial burgh. Work started to extend it on 16th June 1906 and the new harbour and dock complex was completed in 1909 when the official opening was carried out by the Earl of Elgin. The first ship planned to use the harbour was to be the SS *Kirkcaldy* owned by linen manufacturer Major HL Stocks, but a sailing ship loaded with timber stole the day slightly by slipping into the harbour first. The harbour extension and dock meant that large cargo ships could come in with raw materials for the town's industries and leave with exports of coal, linoleum, linen, pottery and other manufactured goods.

It was also the setting off point for the fleet of whaling ships such as *Viewforth*, *Caledonia*, *Triad*, *Regalia*, and *Hecla*. It was a hard and dangerous way to earn a living: *Lord Gambier*, *Abram* and *Chieftain* were trapped in the ice although their crews were eventually rescued. Reports of their cargoes make uncomfortable reading today; in 1833 the whalers brought home 900 tons of whale oil and 60 tons of whalebone. But in those days it was seen as a necessary employment; and indeed a local recollection from the 1850s records that the school children in Pathhead got a day's holiday from school "to see the sailing ships go off to Greenland" – no doubt crewed by their fathers and older brothers.

The growth of industry in Kirkcaldy was mainly due to the investment and foresight of men such as Sir Michael Barker Nairn, Provost Michael Beveridge, Major Harris Stocks, and Robert Philp. As well as providing work such as manufacturing linoleum, linen and weaving for thousands of the townsfolk, these 'captains of industry' as they were known used some of their wealth to improve the educational, health and social life of the district. Sir Michael Barker Nairn for instance gave funds to enlarge the burgh school and gift the cottage hospital; John Nairn erected the Museum building as a commemoration of the First World War and later extended the building to include a public library, reading room and children's library; Provost Michael Beveridge left £50,000 to Kirkcaldy Town Council for a public park and for a library and hall to add to the newly-built Adam Smith Halls; Sir Michael Nairn gave the grounds of Dysart House to the town for use as a public park; and John Hunter gifted St. Brycedale House 'for the benefit of aged and infirm men and women who were not in receipt of Parish Council relief'. Major Harris Stocks, owner of Kirkcaldy and London Shipping Company, built the Victoria Hall for the use of the 4th Company of the Boys Brigade; and linen manufacturer Robert Philp established three schools in Kirkcaldy and one in Kinghorn for poor and disadvantaged children. It's fitting then that many of these men are still remembered in the town's history.

Other notable citizens were also born in Kirkcaldy and many of these made their mark not only in the town but throughout the world. Adam Smith, born in the town's High Street and baptised in 1723, was a hugely influential political economist and many of his principles set out in his book *The Wealth of Nations* are still embraced today. Engineer and inventor Sir Sandford Fleming was born in 1827 and emigrated to Canada when he was 17. He was surveyor and engineer in charge for the proposed Canadian Pacific Railway and devised the modern system of standard time and time zones. In more recent times David Steel MP, first presiding officer of the Scottish Parliament, and former Prime Minister Gordon Brown whose father was minister at St. Brycedale Church, are also Kirkcaldy natives.

Kirkcaldy Civic Society, which was established in 1974, has devoted years of time and energy in researching the history of the town. They have published several booklets, erected plaques on the site of important or interesting buildings, and led regular walkabouts around the town to pass on their knowledge to the public.

Another famous son was world famous architect Robert Adam, who was born in Gladney House, a 17th century mansion house which stood in the Links area off Bute Wynd. A large three-storey building with distinctive curved gables at each corner and a garden stretching down to the shores of the Forth, it declined sharply after the family moved to Edinburgh, where Robert Adam went on to design many beautiful classical buildings such as Register House, Mellerstain, Airthrey Castle, Alnwick Castle and Culzean Castle. The house itself probably changed hands several times and became a 'model' lodging house for homeless families. By 1890 there were 60 people living in what by then were dreadful and squalid conditions. In 1927 plans were in hand to demolish the building and permission to do this was requested to HM Office of Works; this was agreed with the suggestion from the Ancient Monuments Board for Scotland that 'certain stones should be retained as a reminder and memorial of the house. If still in existence, the cannon ball embedded in the front of the house should be preserved in its surrounding masonry along with other detail fragments.'

Sad as it was that such a historic building was to be demolished, it was apparent that by that time there was little alternative. But it is difficult now to justify the thinking behind the demolition some 25 years later of a stately and unique Adam-designed house which stood just a few blocks away from Gladney. Viewforth Towers was a beautiful 14-roomed mansion complete with a three-storey tower, distinctive rounded rooms, large wine cellars and a carved ceiling in black, green and gold. The reason for its demolition was to provide space for badly needed new housing in the area: the then Kirkcaldy Town Clerk was quoted in the *Fifeshire Advertiser* as saying: "The development plan shows that this is an area needing comprehensive redevelopment: we cannot do this and leave a building like that in the redevelopment we propose to do." So in this brave new world of the 1950s, 'a building like that' disappeared in the name of progress to be replaced by blocks of eight-storey flats.

Many other old buildings have gone: mostly from necessity to improve what must have been dire living conditions with little sanitation or modern conveniences, but some alas in line with 'improvements' made country wide when historic buildings or indigenous architecture were flattened in the name of progress. But a careful observer can still see some of the old buildings and architectural features which have escaped the developers: it's just a case of looking round, looking up and recognising some of the original stonework, pillars and arches which still grace the town today.

High Street is pictured in the days when the trams were a vital part of the traffic system. The frontage of the George Hotel can be seen on the right next to the old Town Hall with its lamp standards outside the door. The Town Hall premises included prisoners' cells at the rear, and weekly corn markets were held every Saturday outside on the High Street. Bell Inn Wynd on the left is still in existence although most of the old privately owned shops have been replaced by larger stores or commercial premises.

This view of the High Street is taken from the junction of Kirk Wynd looking west, showing the Gaumont Cinema and Restaurant. It was formerly the Rialto and had a regular Saturday morning club for its young patrons with the popular serial *Flash Gordon* which always ended with a cliff-hanger. It went on fire some years ago and the site was cleared to build new shops. The Clydesdale and North of Scotland Bank later became the Clydesdale Bank which recently closed its premises in Kirkcaldy. The High Street at this time was still open to traffic in both directions; this changed first to a one-way system and is now a pedestrian zone.

Page 5

Page 6

Page 8

Page 9

The east end of the Promenade was a favourite spot for a leisurely stroll, with some youngsters taking a paddle in the water and several factory chimneys visible in the background. Seafield Tower can just be made out in the far distance and to the left of that, the remaining remnants of what was intended to be a grand scheme in the late 1800s to the early 1900s to build a large harbour and dock. This was meant to take steamers, cargo vessels and fishing boats, with plans for 16 acres of railway sidings where between 12,000 and 15,000 tons of coal could be stored in trucks ready to be shipped out. The grand plan however never came to fruition with only a few reminders of the construction work still left today.

St. Clair Street was named after the St. Clair family, the Earls of Rosslyn, who once owned huge estates in Dysart and Kirkcaldy until the 5th Earl who had a heady lifestyle of gambling, race-horses and beautiful women went bankrupt and had to sell up the entire estate in 1896. This old image shows an early car although horse-drawn traffic was still popular and the tram cars were coming into service. A few of the old houses still exist in some form although many now have incorporated commercial premises and shops into the ground floor.

The houses in Oswald Road may have a picturesque charm for those looking back today, but they would have been well below modern standards with outdoor sanitation probably shared by several families, and little or no home comforts. Most of the families living in them worked in one of the three nearby potteries. The houses were demolished years ago and a modern well-planned estate of houses now stands in the area.

The Adam Smith Hall and Beveridge Free Library were opened in 1899 with the generous legacy of £50,000 from Provost Michael Beveridge, one of the leading floorcloth manufacturers in Kirkcaldy. The Adam Smith Hall originally seated 1,300 while the Beveridge Hall which was intended for smaller gatherings accommodated 300 and included a free library and reading room. Andrew Carnegie of Skibo Castle officially opened the building on 11th October 1899 and also presented a fine organ for the hall. Now operated by Fife Cultural Trust, it continues to host a variety of entertainments.

Page 10

Page 11

Page 13

Page 14

Kirkcaldy Burgh School was built in 1843 to replace an earlier school in Hill Street where Thomas Carlyle once taught. Originally a single storey building with Grecian-type pillars on the front, it was extended 50 years later with funding from linoleum magnate Michael Barker Nairn and the facade of the ground floor was incorporated into the building. After a series of alterations, a modern complex which is now Fife College stands on part of the site. The distinctive little curved building on the right is still there.

The stylish Burton's building on the corner of the High Street and Whytescauseway must be one of the few Kirkcaldy shops still with its original exterior. This image which dates from the early 1960s shows shop fronts including Brighter Homes, Grieve's and Bata, which are all now just memories. By this time, the trams and cobbles had disappeared but the two-way traffic system was still in operation. This part of the High Street is now a pedestrianised zone with few if any privately owned shops remaining.

The railway came to Kirkcaldy in 1847 when the first passenger station with its distinctive canopy was opened. Its freight traffic played a huge part in the town's industries and it was no accident that two of the main floorcloth factories owned by Michael Nairn and Co. Ltd. and Barry Ostlere and Shepherd Ltd. were built beside the railway line for convenient freight transport. The days of the steam trains on the line have long since gone although special trips have been made by the Union of South Africa and (in 2016) the iconic Flying Scotsman. The station itself has been modernised and upgraded over the years with new buildings and facilities.

The kilns belonging to pottery manufacturers David Methven and Sons were a landmark in the Links area. The firm produced a huge amount of domestic pottery including Auld Heatherware which was decorated by sponge painting, and Abbotsford Ware which was similar in many respects to the more celebrated Wemyss Ware – which now commands huge prices – made by Fife Pottery in the Gallatown. When the pottery closed down in the early 1930s, the kilns were demolished and the Raith Ballroom and then Raith Cinema stood on the site to be replaced by the current Rhema Church.

Page 15

Page 16

Page 18

Page 19

Sailors' Walk, Kirkcaldy's oldest house, was probably built in the 15th century and was saved from the threat of demolition in 1934 when a forward-looking committee launched a public appeal. It was taken over by the National Trust for Scotland which began the task of restoration which was eventually completed after the Second World War. Some amazing original features were uncovered including a wooden ceiling decorated with fish and flowers, a wooden bed which slid into a stone recess, fleur-de-lis and thistles in plaster on the walls and beams inscribed with Biblical texts. The buildings now house a variety of commercial concerns.

The houses in Nether Street in the 1900s had an attractive appearance with cottages which had traditional pantile roofs and two-storey houses built on a gradual slope. A redevelopment programme took place around the 1960s, and the building in the right foreground which was the nurses' home for the nearby Cottage Hospital is the only original block still remaining. St. Clair Tavern on the corner of St. Clair Street, and once locally known as Skittle Alley, is still a distinctive landmark.

Tullis Stables in Tollbooth Street supplied horse-drawn cabs for the townsfolk and when required, hearses. The line-up in the photograph includes owner George Tullis with one of his horses, a telegraph boy on the extreme right, a blacksmith with his leather apron and tools, and the gent in the top hat on the left was probably a coachman. The building was originally Kirkcaldy Free Church and when its congregation moved on to build St. Brycedale Church in 1881, the building was taken over by a firm of undertakers before being incorporated into Marks and Spencer's store. The exterior is still recognisable and a plaque marking its history has been installed on the old front door.

Port Brae Cinema was situated at the east end of the High Street, opening in 1913 as one of the many picture houses in Kirkcaldy which were well patronised in the golden age of the cinema. A 1928 street directory includes the Opera House – later renamed the Regal Cinema and then the ABC – the Palace in Whytescauseway, the Palladium, the Rialto and the Rio in St. Clair Street. When the Port Brae cinema closed down in the 1940s, the site was redeveloped several times and is currently a car wash.

Page 20

Page 21

Page 23

Page 24

Port Brae looking east around 1930. The building in the background was St. James' Church (originally Port Brae Church) which was demolished in the 1970s to make way for road widening and car parking. There is also Gillies' furniture shop, the Army Club, and (on the left) seed merchant David Hutchison. These shops are no longer there but the building on the left with the distinctive stone cladding still operates as licensed premises.

Kirkcaldy Harbour was a busy port as early as the 16th century when King James V of Scotland sailed from there to France in 1536 to bring back his bride Madeleine de Valois. The Marquis of Montrose was taken from Kirkcaldy by ship in May 1650 to face execution in Edinburgh two days later. The harbour played a vital part in the town's industries, particularly for importing cork and exporting the finished product for the linoleum trade. As the town's industries decreased, harbour trade dwindled; one of the contributory factors was when cement for the building industry was manufactured in Dunbar instead of being imported, and the Coastline cement ships (centre of the image with chevron on its funnel) were no longer needed. After being virtually deserted by large vessels for many years, the harbour trade re-opened in 2013 with long low ships coming in regularly to deliver wheat from home and abroad to Carr's huge modern flour mill at the foot of the Path.

Heggie's Wynd, named after a linen manufacturer, was typical of the series of short wynds leading from Links Street down to what was then Sands Road and is now the Promenade. This view shows the three-storey houses known as the Old Mill with the houses of Page's Pend to the left. The tall chimney was part of Abbotshall Foundry and it, along with all the other buildings, were demolished in the late 1930s as part of a demolition programme in the Links which carried on until the 1950s and 1960s. The street name is still there with a car showroom on one side and the Philp Hall on the corner.

The distinctive Swan Memorial building on the corner of Kirk Wynd and High Street was built in 1895 at a cost of £3,500 as a memorial to Provost Don Swan. For many years it was the headquarters of Kirkcaldy YMCA whose members previously met in the Hunter Hall before moving to their current premises in Valley Gardens. Currently a charity shop, the building retains the stone with the inscribed Swan Memorial which can still be seen at the top of the building just below the pediment.

Page 25

Page 26

Page 28

Page 29

Commercial Street in the 1920s and 30s was typical of the time when shops and businesses were mostly privately owned, including the upholsterer and painter and decorator which are pictured on the left. The distinctive curved building on the corner of Broad Street with advertisements for fresh butter and new-laid eggs housed the Buttercup Dairy. This building was the very first shop set up in 1904 by the Buttercup Dairy Company which built up 250 branches throughout the UK over 25 years. Happily the building has survived throughout the years, though with different proprietors, as has the Pathhead Hall which can be seen on the right.

The tramway system ran from 1903 until May 1931 and was a source of great pride to the townsfolk as it was the first town in Fife and indeed one of the first in the UK to run trams. Many local businesses took up the opportunity to advertise on the sides of the tramcars. This junction was often the scene of congestion as one tram route went straight along the High Street and the other turned at almost right angles up Whytescauseway. Surprisingly, given the amount of demolition which has been carried out in the High Street, the building with the triangular points on the roof is still there today.

The corner of St. Clair Street and Junction Road was a busy place around the 1930s as it was one of the major tram routes, servicing not only the people who lived in the area but also those who worked in the many factories which can be seen in the background. Although the factory buildings and their industries have now all gone and are replaced with modern housing, the building on the right with its distinctive turret has survived the demolition squads.

Bridge Street in the early 1900s was part of a busy industrial area with a spinning mill on each side of the road and a brewery. Robert Philp's linen mill, powered by water from the Tiel Burn, was on the left and was later used to house Hogarth's flour mill. When the building was demolished to make way for new housing, a plaque was erected on the site and the huge mill spindle socket which was recovered intact was built into the boundary wall. Hendry's West Spinning Mill on the other side of Bridge Street which stood empty for many years has been sensitively restored and converted into the Foyer, which houses housing voluntary and charitable organisations.

Page 30

Page 31

Page 33

Page 34

Kirk Wynd is one of Kirkcaldy's most historic streets, with the Old Kirk which was consecrated in 1244 at the top of the hill. It was the scene of a tragedy in 1828 when Edward Irving came to preach: his reputation was so high that so many people crowded into the back gallery – said to have been shoddily built – collapsed. The falling beams killed two members of the congregation and another 26 people were crushed to death in the rush for the exit. The church is now under the care of Kirkcaldy Old Kirk Trust which preserves its heritage. Writer Thomas Carlyle lodged in the house on the right with the outside stair when he taught for two years at the Burgh School which stood opposite at the junction with Hill Street. His house was demolished and replaced by the Trustees Savings Bank and is now a pub. The building on the left which was once houses and a decorator's business is currently the offices of the local newspaper.

Michael Nairn's classical red sandstone offices were landmarks at the top of the Path and some of the company's linoleum factories were established on both sides of the street with a walkway for workers linking them across the road. An early reminiscence from an elderly man who lived in the area at the time recalled that many of the old houses were demolished to make room for the factory and the offices. The office block itself was knocked down some years ago and its one time neighbour, then called Old Dunnikier House and the former mansion house of the Laird of Dunnikier, has been carefully preserved and is now Path House which is occupied as a doctor's surgery.

Gladney House in Bute Wynd was the birthplace of world famous architect Robert Adam who was responsible for some of the most dignified neo-classical buildings and interiors in the country. After the family moved to Edinburgh, Gladney House deteriorated and was latterly a lodging house which eventually became overcrowded and insanitary. This rare image shows the start of its demolition in 1931 as part of the Kirkcaldy Improvement Scheme. One of Kirkcaldy Civic Society's plaques has been placed near the site.

The Cottage Hospital in Nether Street was gifted to the town by linoleum manufacturer Michael Barker Nairn. It was opened in November 1890 and was seen as a welcome step forward in the care of the sick, with an extension added later with distinctive circular wards. A contemporary account of the building said: "It has male and female wards, each containing nine beds. There are also matron's and nurses' rooms, an operating room, and a children's ward, all of which are well lighted and ventilated. The heating is done by means of hot water pipes which run under the flooring. Over the main entrance facing the street there is this inscription: 'I was sick and ye visited me'." When the Victoria and Hunter Hospitals were built, there was no need for the smaller hospital and it was demolished in 1985 with a small estate called the Kyles built on the site.

Page 35

Page 36

Page 38

Page 39

Linktown was originally a separate burgh from Kirkcaldy until its amalgamation with its neighbour in 1876. Under a succession of improvement schemes, many of the historic buildings in and around Links Street were demolished including the building with the curved outside stair which (along with its adjoining jail) housed the Baron Baillie, law officer and judge. Prisoners' cells were situated behind the stair and there was a bell on the roof which was rung on special occasions including the Armistice at the end of the First World War. Although many of the improvements were necessary, Gladney House and a beautiful circular Adam designed mansion, Viewforth Towers, were sadly also demolished. The nearby Market Place was the traditional site for stalls and side shows of the annual Links Market before they moved on to the Prom along with the larger rides. Most of the old houses and wynds have been replaced with modern homes.

The Path was always a very steep incline firstly for horse-drawn vehicles and then for the tramcars. A narrow thoroughfare with no pavements, it was the site of several fatal accidents: in 1837 the minister of Kirkcaldy Parish Church, the Rev. Martin, was thrown from his gig when descending the Path and was killed. In 1888 the driver of a horse-drawn van was thrown on to the road and fatally injured, and on another occasion a schoolboy was trying to pass a loaded cart which was swaying from side to side and was crushed against the wall. The Path was widened and improved several times from 1863 onwards with the worst bend in the road straightened out. Carr's flour mill can be seen on the left of the modern image with the facade of Nairn's St. Mary's canvas factory in the centre background.

Victoria Road is pictured here with an interesting contrast of the new tramway system and the traditional horse-drawn vehicles passing the thriving furniture factory belonging to AH Mackintosh. The firm produced very fine pieces and exhibited work at the Paris Furniture Exhibition in 1879 and even further afield in Australia at the Sydney Exhibition in 1880. Their marquetry panels and furniture were fitted in the *Queen Mary* which was launched in 1934. The Mackintosh family lived in the nearby house, currently the Victoria Hotel, where there is a commemorative plaque. The former factory site is now occupied by office buildings.

Ravenscraig Park had a fine example of a working floral clock, less known perhaps than the one in Edinburgh's Princes Street but a source of interest to visitors to the park. The park itself was originally part of the Earl of Rosslyn's estates, but when the 5th Earl went bankrupt the mansion house and policies were bought by Sir Michael Nairn in 1896. Nairn, in one of his many public spirited gestures, gifted the park to the town so that people could enjoy its amenities and enjoy the fine views of the Forth. Although the floral clock has now gone, the park is still beautifully kept by Fife Council's Parks Department with a wide display of varying flower beds.

Page 40

Page 41

Page 43

Page 44

Mid Street, parallel to Commercial Street (originally known as Back Street) was one of the oldest streets in Pathhead, then a separate burgh from Kirkcaldy and the site of the annual Pathhead Market. An 1850s account said "Mid Street had many outside stairs and porches on to the pavements. Most of the houses were thatched and one of the old one-storey houses at the west end had a stable at one end with a family living at the other: the roof fell in and the horse escaped but was found in the country unhurt. The street had two pump wells and two draw wells, but the wooden well at the west end was not used for cooking as it had rather a peculiar taste, perhaps of its proximity to the West Burying Ground." Modern homes have replaced most of the old buildings.

Kirkcaldy's Sheriff Court, originally the County Buildings, was opened in May 1894 at a cost of £9,000. The weekly Sheriff Court was held every Wednesday, and County – as distinct from Burgh – Courts were also held there, with the Sheriff Clerk's office on the premises. A contemporary guide book describes the building as "being in the Scottish Baronial style of architecture with a square tower in the centre with a circular tower, conical roof and weathervane, and battlement on top. It forms the best specimen of the castellated style of architecture in the district and the plans were prepared by Mr. Gillespie of St. Andrews acting under the instructions of Fife County Council." The building still stands today with a modern glass and stone extension.

Work on sinking the shaft at Seafield Colliery began in 1954, with the pit taking the coal from the huge deposits under the Forth and employing around 2,000 miners at its peak. The colliery's design with its twin towers was described in a contemporary Kirkcaldy guidebook as "so dignified that in certain lights and from certain angles they remind one of such towers as one finds in a cathedral town." A disaster in May 1973 caused by a massive roof fall under the Forth killed five miners and injured four more. In 1980 it was linked under the Forth with the Frances Colliery in Dysart, but Seafield was closed down in March 1988 and the whole complex was demolished a year later. An estate of modern houses with a view of the Forth now occupies the site.

Thomas Reilly's Salt Works were situated at the foot of Coal Wynd next to the harbour and would have provided a flourishing business when salt was used as a preservative as well as for flavouring. The 1885 Trades Directory shows that the previous owner was James White, and by 1894 it was listed as belonging to Mrs. Thomas Reilly, one of the women pictured in this image which was taken around 1912. The salt would have been made through evaporation from the salt pans on the shore, and possibly later by refining rock salt. The site is now a car park.

Page 45

Page 46

Page 48

Inside Back Cover

Pathhead United Free Church stood at the foot of St. Clair Street where the Cottage Hospital can just be seen to the left. The church was the subject of an interdict in 1905 when the Court of Session granted the 'Wee Free' Church in Pathhead the right of occupancy to the building. The UF congregation had to vacate their building and marched to the nearby public hall to hold their services there. The church building was demolished in 1963 as part of a modernisation scheme and multi-storey flats now stand on the site.